Dear Friends
Far and Near

Dear Friends Far and Near

POEMS

FRITZ JAENSCH

DEAR FRIENDS FAR AND NEAR
POEMS

Scripture quotations from the Holy Bible, King James Version (Authorized Version). First published in 1611. Quoted from the KJV Classic Reference Bible.

iUniverse books may be ordered through booksellers or by contacting:

iUniverse
1663 Liberty Drive
Bloomington, IN 47403
www.iuniverse.com
1-800-Authors (1-800-288-4677)

ISBN: 978-1-5320-5283-5 (sc)
ISBN: 978-1-5320-5284-2 (e)

Library of Congress Control Number: 2018907956

Print information available on the last page.

iUniverse rev. date: 07/30/2018

Fritz Jaensch was born on August 2, 1934, in Frankfurt am Main, Germany. In 1936 his father, Wilhelm (designer, photographer, Bauhaus student), and his mother, Hella (a learned librarian)—both unemployed—took him back to their home city, Königsberg, in Germany's East Prussia. Here Wilhelm found work as a policeman, while his widowed mother, Helene, welcomed the family to her home. It was only a block from Fritz's mother's childhood home, and it was no more than three blocks distant from Mrs. Berwaldt's home, whose daughter, Hannah Arendt, had just fled Nazi Germany. But Hannah's mother was unable to follow. Until she, too, managed to escape, her daughter's friend Hella, Fritz's mother, visited her as often as she could.

In 1939, she managed to leave behind the land of deadly persecution that Germany had become, especially for Jewish and Romani people and the handicapped, and their friends. The United States took her and her daughter, Hannah, in as refugees.

In May 1939, Fritz's sister Johanna was born. Five months thereafter, the Gestapo came to the door and took their mother away. His mother's cousin Hedel took the children in. Now Fritz had two mothers—all that love. But now came the Great War that set loose all the horrors arising from the merciless grasp for power.

Through all this time, Fritz's life proceeded as if charmed, as expressed in lines from Psalm 91: "A thousand may fall at your side / and ten thousand at Your right hand; / but it shall not come near you."

The war came and went. And now the family became acquainted with starvation. That experience, verified in Holy Writ, prompted Fritz to choose farming as his vocation. With no farm to inherit, he hoped to be able to earn a farm in the United States. Hannah Arendt sponsored his immigration in the spring of 1956. He went to work on a dairy farm in California.

In the years to follow, his intellectual inheritance began to assert itself. His parents told him, "Fritz, you are called to do more than milk cows. You read Shakespeare to your children." Friends at church saw the same and recommended that he go to school. Taking the advice to heart, he went to high school, attended college for his BA in history and an MA in European history, and continued work in a PhD program at the University of California, Berkeley. All the while he did the work of a farmhand and did building maintenance—a wealth of learning, a life lived with gratitude.

Foreword

Fritz Jaensch and I have been close friends for many years. Together Fritz and I have been through the book-writing process twice and are now starting on our third tour of duty. Throughout this period it has been a treat to enjoy the once or twice monthly creation of a new poem by Fritz. Over the years Fritz's poems have brought me much joy, wonder, and amazement. The joy is based on images evoked by his poems, and the wonder and amazement come from the startling degree to which Fritz's poems combine the wonders of the natural world with the amazement of the spiritual world.

Fritz's poems remind me greatly of the works of Henry David Thoreau. In particular, they remind me of Thoreau's book *A Week on the Concord and Merrimack Rivers*, which explores the wonder of discovering the great variety of flora and fauna along this river watershed northwest of the city of Boston. Clearly Thoreau feels, though he clearly doesn't say it, the hand of God at work within the biological world of the creatures that call these rivers home. Thoreau is masterful at describing the lives of the tiny animal and plants that inhabit these waters. In a few simple words, Thoreau is able to capture the fascinatingly complex lives led by these tiny creatures. Fritz does much the same with his poems. Like Thoreau, Fritz captures in verse the details of the lives led by the small but largely hidden creatures that are usually overlooked by passersby.

Fritz's poems also remind me of Saint Francis of Assisi. The legend of Saint Francis, whether truth or myth, talks of a man who loved and cherished the natural world just as much as he loved and cherished God and the world of spirit. Fritz tells all of us that he, like Saint Francis, loves and cherishes both the natural world of flora and fauna and God's world of the spirit.

Like Henry David Thoreau and Saint Francis before him, Fritz Jaensch profoundly believes, and lives out in his life, the concept that there exists a duality connecting the natural world and the spiritual world. For Fritz, the early bird that shows up on his front lawn in search of its daily worm is as much an actor on life's stage as any Shakespearean. Like in a Shakespearean comedy or tragedy, these little actors are grappling with the meaning and practice of truth in their own miniature worlds.

In many small ways, elements of C. S. Lewis's, Beatrix Potter's, and J. R. R. Tolkien's works are also mixed into Fritz's poems. That is to say, with a little imagination, it is easy to see how the lives of Fritz's tiny animals reflect the "grand" lives of human beings and the greater spiritual issues we all confront. Within Fritz's poems we see a raptor threatening a mother bird while she sits on the eggs in her nest. The mother bird's plight reminds us of the need for God to deliver us from the terrors and dangers within our own lives. Sometimes Fritz likens the vast migration of butterflies to an insatiable search for the God within us all. For Fritz, the first robin of spring is an announcement of the newly risen Christ, awakening us all to a new world achieved by our victorious God. These little creature actors of the natural world are playing the part of principals within the world of spirit. Hand in hand, the actors of the natural world dance, swing, and turn in time to the music they share with the spiritual principals they are playing.

Allen Sweet, PhD, adjunct professor of electrical engineering, Santa Clara University, Santa Clara, California

Stage of Life

The stage of life is always set.
The props remain in place
But change each morning
When the light arises and

The neighborhood, awake,
Makes ready for the sacrifice
With heartfelt thanks
For beauty, love, and life.

The hawk, the owl, the crows,
Perched in the tall trees,
Have the view I also know
Of land and sea, of joy
And sorrow coming into view,

Arising from earth's continents
And being carried with the wind and
Ocean waves to gently or alarmingly
Rush that news into our bay for you and me.

Unseen but clearly heard
From heights beyond the tall trees
The Word sounds.
I try to translate for the little birds
Their joyful lives' validity
For each assigned responsibility,
Each sign and dot within established law.

1

The brindle-coated sparrow bird
Sent to my home stage here
Comes to the window with an urgent word.
His beak, wings skilled for flight,
And feet secure in letting go and landing,
Bird uses all of these to formulate
The Word created for my apprehending.

Bird spoke with all its energy
The language sent with him to me.
"Let go of 2017.
Be not afraid of what your neighbors fear,
But turn to me," says the son of Mary and Joseph,
Man of earth.
"Have faith and follow me, and so
The Word receive.

The Word,
I AM,
Am Jesus, Son of God,
Come to earth for you to hear and see
And live."

January 3, 2018

Silken Cloth

Smooth as a silken cloth,
the eventide delivers peace,
invited at the Golden Gate
to harmonize the evensong
of slowly rising setting waves,
the waning sunlight, waxing moon,
accompanied by music of the spheres.
So with our prayers and blessings laden,
they westward ply into the perilous seas.

The bay itself is silently
attentive to the slowly parting day.
Who would have thought
its silence could have stopped
the quaking earth's typhoons,
heartrending cruel wars, a tsunami's
worth of suffering children's tears,
all rushing at this California coast,
until they reach this San Francisco Golden Gate.
Those storms arisen from the warlike sea,
here now calmed down, speak with a mother's voice
the Word.

Be still, proud waves.
This is the moment of the end of strife,
the coming of peace that passes understanding,
the love that heals the heart of all created life.

These waters washing silently to shore
bring with them all the tears
that ever have been cried,
yours, too, and mine.
They shall be consecrated here,
the living water, precious blood,
our offering of gratitude and love:
Lehayim! To life!
Thanks be to God.

Redemption: Advent Ante Porta

A waning moon,
a mellow shining shipshape, is
illumining the morning sky.
I cannot fail to see above it
Leonardo's blue and
beautiful Madonna.

Her feet are resting
on this bright and peaceful vessel,
bearing Christ
through all the folds
of universe and sky—
royal Messiah
to our pitifully war-plagued home,
the earth.

From here our woeful cries
rise up to him and her:
Maria, help us!

Bear your man-child
in your womb,
God's chosen vessel,
earthward,
to redeem the human soul,
and all creation with us
by your love.
Thanks be to God.
Thanks be to you.

Dear friends far and near: My poem is a prayer, a supplication with all of you in mind.

My simplest rule for prayer is this: Say what is wanting. Ask for that to be supplied. Give thanks for what you are receiving.

There is a prayer I learned when I was very little and could not yet speak English. It goes like this: *Lieber Gott mach mich fromm, dass ich in den Himmel komm.* Amen.

Here is the same prayer in English: Dear God, make me devout so that I get to heaven. Amen.

We can let the word *amen* stand for "thanks" because what is wanting is always supplied. Make it simple, and keep it positive.

Apprehension

Strangely devoid of creatures is
the outlook through the window
frame. The stoop, the stage I have,
gives me no clue if they hide
in the eucalyptus branches,
golfing meadows. Closer in?
Perhaps a little farther out
in neighbors' garden hedges or
the vegetable gardens of the house?
Obscured is morning light under a veil of clouds.

I miss the robin families, now pairing up
for spring. Also the crows, my neighbors,
and the squirrels, raccoons, and skunks.
It's been so long since I last heard
the doves' and blackbirds' songs.
They fail to populate my stage out front,
remaining absent from the line of sight,

but they do send me vague messages I like.
I know the themes and rhythms of their songs
out from the distant towns around the bay,
where things are now afoot that might
scare or attract them—I don't know.
Details elude my senses.

The morning air is peaceful and so still.
No leaf, no branch, is stirring.

Rain in the forecast for the afternoon.
Perhaps another storm?
I do not know. None of my furred
or winged actors are onstage
to tell me so. Their absence is
the word I have to meditate upon.

The Word I pray and meditate upon,
the Word of Love assured.
My faith is anchored in your love,
O High and Holy One.

You give us hope!
I give you thanks
with all I am.
Amen.

My dear friends far and near: Here is a prayer thought: Lord, thy kingdom come. May thy will guide all our thoughts and actions on this earth, the realm of our responsibility. Amen.

May the Holy One embrace all of us with love and grant us peace.

Surprise

From out of darkness
I hear voices whispering,
"Beware the ides of March."

I, with the first light of the day,
witness a miracle:

camellias opening to the morning wind,
swaying, dancing with smiles of spring.
And honeybees are harvesting
the blossoms in this month of Valentine,
pregnant with hope and joy
and love divine.
Thanks be to God.

Alamedacare 2

Dear Friends:

Today's gospel reading is taken from Jesus's Sermon on the Mount. It is called that because when the Lord noticed that more and more people were drawn to him, he decided that the time had come to teach his closest friends the rules of the kingdom of heaven. So he went up on a mountain ahead of them. He found a suitable place where they could hear him. There he sat down and taught them.

He taught them first the beatitudes, the blessings that come with an attitude that favors people with empathy for the weak, the powerless, and the persecuted. Jesus then followed up with lessons comparing the traditional demands set down in the Torah, the law Moses received from God on Mount Sinai. This is the law Jesus came among us to fulfill.

Now as we first read these instructions, we cannot help but be taken aback by the sheer difficulty of the demand. The Lord tells us life was tough under the old rules. "But wait until you hear my rules. They will be even more difficult to follow," he essentially says. There is, for instance, the rule against anger. We hear a lot about this rule these days. It is the rule against bullying in school but also in the workplace. Wherever we people are brought together, we can create happiness or misery, depending on what we think.

Here is what the Lord explains: "You have heard the commandment imposed on your forefathers, 'You shall not commit murder, every murderer shall be liable to judgment.' But what I say to you is this: Everyone who grows angry with his brother shall be liable to judgment; any man who uses abusive language toward his brother shall be answerable to the judicial assembly; and if he holds his brother in contempt, he risks the fires of gehenna" (Matthew 25:21–22).

That warning reminds me of a warning sign I passed on Tunnel Road in Berkeley where there is a sharp bend in the road. It reads, "Do not even think of parking here!" And that is the clue to what Jesus is teaching us here: Your thoughts are as real as your deeds. Think a vengeful thought against your neighbor––you might as well have picked up a stick to beat him with it. Thoughts can injure.

But thoughts can also heal and help and establish peace, joy, and friendship.

So then let us think good of one another. Let us use our thoughts to create an atmosphere of friendliness and healing. Good thoughts are the bright light the Lord has given us to make the world a better place.

Let that light shine!

Meditation presented to the people at Alameda Care Center

Dear friends far and near: I send this to you with heartfelt blessings.

Ode to a Wilted Rose

Like red-rimmed golden silk,
you swayed and jubilantly
danced your joy through
rain and storm that elsewhere
from the branches ripped
your sisters, threw them into silt
that washed around the roots'
imperiled life.

But rose roots, planted firmly
in the rain-soaked ground,
held fast the rose, beloved
of the bee, communion sheltering
among camellia leaves and
sister blossoms by the house.

They watched with admiration how
your red-rimmed golden petals'
peerless beauty unfolded on the highest
bow in wind and thunderous rain—
unfolded out their highest praise
of beauty unto God.

The storm abated. Hummingbirds
returned. One was so taken
by the glory of your perfect dance,
he touched your aura's
light impeccable and danced

your life eternal,
Mary Magdalen,
to its fulfillment
in the arms of
Jesus Christ,
your friend, your most beloved.

How bright the glow
of that accomplished love.

Interlude at Crab Cove

Who would have thought
We'd see the sunshine guild,
The Crab Cove's water so,
Making its rippled wavelets
Shine like silver pearls scooped up
And broadcast over all the
Living gauze of liquid blue
That keeps the city, the bridge,
And the mountain out of view?

Over the rain-soaked meadow grass
Two mallard ducks, approaching,
Grant me a recognizing glance.
The female then walks to inspect
A movement in the knoll of grass.

The mallard male stands back,
Watching his agitated mate.
A sound arises from the knoll,
One I'd never heard from a duck before.

Now both let up and walk away.
As from among the boulders walks
A squirrel, which leisurely
Begins to graze the herbs
That grow around my feet
Below my observation seat.
Squirrel was the author of that sound.

The sun has meanwhile moved
More westerly toward the end of day.
Squirrel must have had a thought
And ran with it, off and away.

The tide, done rising now, is settling
Into the stillness of perfected day.
Terns, gulls, and pipers fly
Once more their evening round
To exercise their wings and pipe
And sing once more their song.
Then, landing on the harbor rocks,
They jostle before settling down.

The tide turns and starts going out.
Good is the evening on its westward way.
Blest is the parting of the day
That angels in this sacred twilight
Hand to God.

February 17, 2017

My dear friends far and near: Nothing is eaten as hot as it comes off the stove. I don't remember where I first heard this proverb, but it has proved very helpful at times in my life when untimely emerging threats have raised the specter of fear.

At such times the proverb tends to remind me of the Holy One who walks with each and every one of us, turning fear into love, walking with us each step of each day.

I want to share that with you all.

Peace, the Word

The sun bequeathed
the water and the land
to mind and to preserve
the greening of the earth.

Now in the evening after
storm-tossed nights and days,
we see the resurrection of the light.
Like slowly sailing ships the clouds'
dark gray along their bottom keel.
Bright golden superstructures sway,
arrayed against the vast blue sky and sea.

They carry light like freight,
and in that freight concealed
are artists: sculptors, carvers
chiseling with unseen hands
the bison, birds, and bears
that roam our forests and
star-spangled prairie lands.

And animals that formerly roamed here
as dinosaurs we ourselves have been,
as well as those we not as yet have seen
approaching us from futureward,
just floating by, just now, just here,
as this observer's thoughts and dreams
in dreamscapes of these clouds appear.

The wavelets of the San Francisco Bay
stream from the north toward the south
against the tide that's drawing out
beneath the westward wind that blows
past city, bridge, and mountain slopes
toward our Alameda coast,
where people on their evening walks
follow their dogs and, with their friends,
exchange their friendly talk.

The Word is peace.
O thank you, Lord.
Peace is your Word
that echoes in my heart.

Dear Friends far and near: These poems I wrote in 1993 and -94. "From where the sun of my earth-days now stands," they likely end up in the re-cycle bin. But you might like them, therefore I share them with best of thoughts your way -- Fritz --

The Stage
+
The starlight fades
before the rising day,
The air is not as clear
as Eve and Adam first perceived it.
The stage is ready
for the first descent.
We're washing windows
at the Watergate.

The view is clear enough to see
the Berkeley hills in back.
Out there, stage left, are
bridge, the City and, alas,
the smoggy hazy atmosphere.
Stage right is Angel Island,
Shark town and the headland's end.
Ahead the ocean and the sky.
My inner sense of wonder longs
to stay this moment's light of day.

But duty-bound
we must descend and work:
Three men on stage,
to wash the windows down,
and clarify the content
of this office building roof to ground.
For all the world
which claims the power over us
must pass our muster
and our cleaning work.
There's GE Capital
and US Mental Health.
One health insurance
limits lovelessly our care.
Computer drives
say who shall be or not.
All people in there
serving wealthy gods.
Some-- do they care?
I wonder: do they know?

Wednesday, March 08, 2017

21

Dear friends far and near: These are poems I wrote in 1993 and 1994, "from where the sun of my earth days now stands." They likely will end up in the recycle bin. But you might like them. Therefore I share them, with the best of thoughts sent your way.

The Stage

The starlight fades
before the rising day.
The air is not as clear
as Eve and Adam first perceived it.
The stage is ready
for the first descent.
We're washing windows
at the Watergate.

The view is clear enough, allowing us to see…
the Berkeley hills in back.
Out there, stage left, are
the bridge, the city, and, alas,
the smoggy, hazy atmosphere.
Stage right is Angel Island,
Sharktown, and the headland's end.
Ahead, the ocean and the sky.
My inner sense of wonder longs
to stay this moment's light of day.

But duty-bound
we must descend and work:
three men onstage
to wash the windows down
and clarify the content
of this office building, roof to ground.
For all the world,
which claims the power over us,

must pass our muster
and our cleaning work.
There's GE Capital
and US Mental Health.
One health insurance
limits lovelessly our care.
Computer drives
say who shall be or not.
All the people in there
serving wealthy gods.
Some—do they care?
I wonder, Do they know?

The glass reflects
to our view the light
that we have seen
before the stage descended,
and in the park below
a couple is holding hands.
How precious, love,
shared over lunch by friends.
"Why don't they do it,"
says one on the stage with us,
"and get it done and over with?"
As if they'd heard,
that couple leaves, annoyed.
So soon is love,
that tender plant, destroyed.

But now we rise again
along the surface of clean glass.
The eye, now freed
from our scrubbing task,

takes stock of life
again with wider vision.
A flock of shorebirds
rises on the wind
and shows sheer love
of life and power in their turning.
And high above them
seagulls ride the wind.
Sheer beauty of their wings
takes jubilantly all my mind
up as the stage ascends
from out of worried work
into clear skies again.

S&F Window Cleaning
October 1994

187: Antialien Law

The rain is here, the frosty nights.
The ewes will soon begin to drop their lambs.
Bold birds of prey already memorize
Last season's pecking of the little lambs.

And overhead the vultures turn and circle 'round.

Last evening at the Safeway in our town
we filled our cart with food that God provides.
And as we went along the well-filled aisles,
around the corner came a Latin family.

I met the kids, the mother, with a smile.
But they switched off their eyes at once and turned away.
What happened?
Things have changed: They're easy prey.
("Most merciful God,
we must confess that we have sinned.")
No longer can they trust; we are to them the vultures.
We have not loved you, Lord, and what is more—
we have not loved our Latin neighbors as ourselves.
We have not loved these children—
have turned them loose.
Their apprehensive eyes are on their mother,
as mine are crying: *Lord, what have I done?*
And overhead the buzzards circle, circle on …

Alameda, November 17, 1994

Desert Morning

The heart is thankful in the quietness
of morning moments of the brightening day,
when all the duties, worries, and anxieties
are in the shining moment held at bay.

You feel adrift without a stated purpose here.
The questioning mind peruses hill and plain.
The worries of the workweek reappear,
But I have seen to mitigate their pain.

What work maintains the mountain's reach,
the valley's humble and receptive floor?
What work for burro and the eagle's sweep?
Is it not given and received before
a human mind can interfere?

Just so, to be content,
my soul, you will have work and its accomplishment,
and joy in the midst of all the drama of this earth,
and love to guide you futureward.
So be content.

L. V., March 19, 1993

The Floods

Rivers overflowing, breaking levies,
and the human violence loosed
from bonds of Russia and America,
break all the bounds and leave us
helpless, vulnerable, when we read
the news and hear the sound
of many waters bearing down
upon the people, flooding
so many eyes with tears.

Nobody mentions all the animals—
except domestic stock—in their
assessment of the floods and bursting
dams, and bombs in Transcaucasian air.
Are we prepared for such a thing?
Are you?

I ask you only this:
What are you willing to give up,
Baruch, my friend, when the invading wall
of steel or water is approaching?

Praise God from whom all blessings flow.
And trials are approaching.
He only asks you to
abandon all and turn to him,
assuring you that he is
sufficient to assuage your pain.

1993
Baruch is Jeremiah's scribe (see Jeremiah 45)
"Old Hundreds," song of praise
Bhagavad Gita

My dear friends far and near: I did not plan to write a poem. It wrote itself—and used my mind to get to the page. And so I share it with you tied together ("to tie"—*religio*) as it is. So with alert circumspection from Friday to Sunday, may the Holy One bless the Sabbath with love.

Spring Song

Good morning, neighbors.
Turn your radios down.
Your TV screens, leave
to their noisy artifices
their shallow, ignorant
slapstick comedies.

We are invited to the quest
for heavenly realms of joy
where the eternal laws reside,
guarding the earth from
humans trying to destroy
what love so carefully created:
light and song to fill the sky,
and heart, and mind.

Out on the lawn
the rose tree wears new leaves.
The morning breeze
adds strength to patience
as the leaves wait for blossoms to appear.

Meanwhile a little bird is landing here,
clothed with a light-gray feather coat
and on its head a round black feather cap.

From the tall trees
another member of the feathered host

sings a new song of
three staccato notes,
followed by pearls
of rolling sounds.

I know that sound.
We called that songster thistle finch,
with red and black and
golden feathers in the face.
The little mother on the nest
is more demurely dressed,
knowing the hawks
do have their eyes on her.
But so has Lord Creator,
who declares,
Springtime has come!
The time to sing your song.

My dear friends far and near: The Lord is risen! Let heart and soul take comfort. In these troubled times, let us be wakeful but also confident. The person we see at the seashore fixing the Easter brunch of fish and bread is the very Word that Mother Miriam brought to light here among us. Wherever our destiny is bound to take us, we shall know him in the breaking of the bread, he whose rule is peace in the midst of mindless warfare.

Quiet Victory

Before the morning clouds
gave way to an even stronger
burst of sunlight echoing
and reverberating "Hallelujah!" shouts,

there was that quiet moment,
sacred stillness, gentle touch
of Mother's healing hand
upon the waking soul-child,
his nightlong struggle from the cross.

Gehenna nightmares, fire, dust,
impending warfare on the earth;
the care for friends who took him
from the tree of earth—finality.

There angels watch and guard
the transubstantiation path
home to the High and Holy One,
while earth is quaking, and rocks break
in overwhelming power of creation,
and Mother's healing presence
blesses us with peace.

★

A little gray smooth-feathered bird,
knowing the story that I also heard,
comes from the rhododendron blossoms

to the stage, the home I share
with winged and rooted life and with
the dancing rose tree on the lawn.
Third-generation offspring
of the single One who danced
ahead of us through hail and winter storm
the earth to life!
Him we are following
through dusk of dawn
into the light of victory with
hallelujahs.

Dear friends far and near: The flow of poetic lines coursing through my mind has slowed, and my poems' content seems to signal a preoccupation with end times. These shadows are proper enough when measured against Psalm 90. But be of good cheer. Ezekiel has the dry-bones dance, the way to life, where beyond the drought the Lord sustains us with clear water, light and life eternal. Hallelujah!

Beyond

The earth is cycling space-time with her
alpha and omega orientation in the search
for each particular assignment
that for all of us is destiny.

The Master's reassuring farewell Word
reveals the upward path ahead of us:
eternal cycling pilgrim's way
of love.

No more returning to the bones of dust.
Let's leave them in the ground and
walk through that dark valley as we must.
Let's help each other out
along that path.

And do be patient, soul. You'll live
to walk and work in your earthen day.
Christ walks ahead of you.
Peace is at home
within your living self.
Conform to love,
creating us and all of life
on earth, and yes,
beyond it on the path
to God.

Dear friends far and near: I am assigned a reading from the book of Acts, the speech of Stephen. That speech is a masterful recapitulation of the Torah and the prophets. My studying those lines brought to my mind a vision I want to share with you. (I hope no bricks start flying in my direction.) The Lord, the Almighty to whom all things are known, is known to forgive and redirect our ways. In him we can confidently place our trust and lives.

Terra Linda

(The Vision of Saint Stephen)

Blue and beautiful
the sky, the ocean waves
united in the worship of
this springtime-brilliant
Sabbath morning, turning
seamlessly united in the
waves and cycles of the
universal light. I see it
dancing upward, outward,
rapidly in rhymes and rhythms
of eternity, eternally belov'd.

The place assigned to me
is solar planet Earth.

Thanks be to God
for such assignment,
whence joyfully I witness
beauty every morning
new, reliably adjusting,
ever onward cycling
progress of creation.

All is included in this dance of
never-ending love.

From where I stand in space and time,
I love you, Lord.
I love your kingdom
and your counsel for my heart and mind.
Yours is the grateful worship
my soul renders to thee
on this bright Sabbath morning.
Amen to thee,
from thee to me.
Amen.

Dear friends far and near: There is in the Christian hymnbook a beautiful song. It starts with the line "My faith looks up to Thee." That prompts the question, How far up? And the answer: up beyond our human self-help arrangements. The thought of this stirred my soul and mind to song. I want to share it with you, with blessings.

Framed by the Window

Curtain, held open allows the world view to come in.
Close to the house the stoop
is filled with nature's beauty.
Here the old man cactus
leans against the flagpole
and enjoys the Maytime
morning air, also the
plants and flowers blossoming.

An unfamiliar sound is heard:
keen e-string startling
trumpet whistle
cleans and clears
the waking morning air.

Chime on the ceiling of the porch welcomes
the hummingbird, the visitor
who flies a bridge path
every day, up to
where tall Australians sway,
and back again to warm
the nest atop the chime.

That keeps us watchers puzzled.
We wait for eggs to hatch
so baby birds may with
their stirring prove their own
and our existence

on this beautiful blue earth.
But they are not forthcoming.

A few steps downward
to the garden plain
my eyes delight in red
and golden roses dancing
in the springtime wind.

Saint Mary and her humble retinue
of blades and blossoms,
green and pink and blue,
with solemn dance
surrounds the sacred mystery,
the red and golden rose.

We, all who walk here, are
the blessed creature-souls
in search of beauty-guided
inner longing, which shows us
the sacred roads
through the familiar paths
we took through streets of our neighborhood,
outward and up
to our longed-for home.

My will does not suffice.
Some fellow souls are interfering
with human-produced annoying noise
of pride-presented innovations:
tin wings and motors, noisy wheels
disturbing our streets and the environment,
filling the air of the surrounding skies.

I lift my eyes in search
of mountain light that
I once knew as part
of Mother's blessing
and launching of
my pilgrimage
to God.

Seek it, and you shall find.
You might have far to roam.
The earth perspective is but small;
the neighborhood is fenced
and claimed as property by law,
mine here, yours there,
the "I have" of the human law,
the "I have not" of human misery.

My eyes extend the view beyond the fenced-in land.
I long to go beyond the point where
the horizon meets the ocean,
blue on blue, sans fence or end,
into realms I always longed for, never knew.
Thy will I cling to, Lord.
My faith will lead me through
along that pilgrimage,
that life in you.
Amen.

Dear friends far and near: Let us take hold of faith to share in these interesting times filled with uncertainty and obscurity. Let us trust the One to whom all hearts are open, to whom all desires are known, and before whom no secrets are hidden. That thought I want to share with you all.

Unseen Things, Present Realities

Bright and foam-capped
dance the choppy wind waves
from the sea into the bay.
I hear them grimly laughing,
also crying, hissing, rolling in
against the Golden Gate.

The towering ocean waves,
the mighty swells and
storms, set them in motion,
bringing to shore alarming news of
warfare, blood, and death a thousandfold.

Cliffs sharp as swords of flint,
with screeching cries of gulls,
cut the statistics of drowned children
into printed columns for delivery
onto the driveways of our neighborhood.

The city's skyline is obscure,
bay waters clothed with fog;
almost invisible, some ships
are anchoring in the city's lee.

The sun shines brightly down on them
with summer warmth and strength,
but it is not strong enough
to penetrate the puzzling veil

making Mount Tamalpais invisible—
also the shipping lanes
to Philippines, to China and Japan.

The evening wind calms down.
The coast birds seek their roosts;
the land birds seek their nests.
We seek the reassuring peace of God.

Darkness descends, although
there's moonlight drifting
over the drifting fog at sea.
Homeward also turn my wheels.
Faith hands all faith–filled thought
with humble thanks
and trust to thee.

Something occurred,
some interference in the
waving over ocean waters,
heat waves over land.

Something particular
disturbed the waving
solar system we rely on.
Come July we raise the flag.

The longest of the days,
turned over as it must,
was barely noticed. Why? Why?
Why do you ask?

Well, there was one particular
unheard-of interference.
Somehow it ended the reliant
waving dance of sea and land.

Not knowing when or where
the action really happened,
I did take note of that event:
The waves regrouped.

The ocean waves remembered, as they should,
their duty to produce the morning fog.
Cool morning waves, and yet

the patriotic flag of summer was left
flagging—and collapsed the erstwhile question,
What has happened with this land?

★

Two friendly crow birds
ply the morning mist
around the gently waving
green leaves of the veining spring.

I missed the spring song
of red robin, missed the flight
of monarch butterflies—welcomed
instead the black-rimmed,
white-winged garden resident
that took the monarch's place,
while monarch had to stay
south of the high forbidding wall of hate.

I miss the owl as well,
and the red-tailed hawk keeping an eye
on squirrels in tall Australian trees.
Also the ground squirrels
all along the bayside promenade.

Nothing along the way is as it used to be.
We oldsters build on hope, and pray:
Thy kingdom come, O Lord.
Give us the help we need.

The kingdom of the heavens
lives within your hearts;

the voice of reassurance can be heard.
Care first and foremost for that verity
I AM,
with all of you along your pilgrims' paths.

Dear friends far and near: When times are turbulent, as are ours, there can be found some quiet moment. No need to frantically hunt or dig for it; just open heart and mind. The gift of quietude will bypass fear-filled circumspection and enter your soul by way of intuition. Let us savor such moments and share them lovingly with all.

Quiet Moments

The moonlight mellowed
as it blended into the rising
light of Sabbath morning.
With neighbors' cars still curbed
and airplanes not yet started,
these morning moments yield
communication space to
neighbor creatures waiting
patiently until the time is theirs
to voice their joyful praise
with their anticipated dancing.

The black-white ambling
butterflies employ their wings
to dance around the single rose,
the beautiful survivor of
a heat wave in the garden.

At this mute moment of
the moonlight's waning,
a gift is given and received.
Life hoped for is enhanced
as precious pearls of moistening dew
entice my neighbor creatures,
breaking into song:
Thanks be to God.
Thanks to
the Holy One.

Aqua Perpetua

Thoughts of my mind,
I set you free,
As in my childhood we
Rode all the horses
Out to pasture for the night,
Took off the halters from their heads,
And turned them loose to seek
Whatever they might find
To eat and digest and
Draw their strength at sunup
For their work.

Was it a particle of mercury
Sent to disturb the ocean's waves,
With heat waves dominating
Coastlands and the
California river valleys?

The land, oppressed, forces
The creatures to adjust,
Until some cooling spark
Adjusts again the balance for the year.

So many of my summer friends
Failed to return from wintering lands.
Now it's too hot to start
The wedding dance of spring.

A flight of geese arise
From nearby watered meadows.
Their rhythmic calls are
Overpowered by the noise
Two raven youngsters make
Protesting the attempt
Their parents undertook
To wean them.

A black-and-gold-winged butterfly
Enjoys the nectar flowing
From purple petals in the garden.
A pair of white-winged
Black-rimmed butterflies
Dance lustily about
Their paradise of many flowers.

Always alone, the squirrel climbs
And hops branch up, branch down,
Inspecting our shelter tree.
Some of the neighbors' cars
Have started and by now are gone.

Warm summer sunshine
Offers us peaceful tableaux
Of greening lawns
Beneath a pale blue sky.

I still miss the monarch's rust-red wings.
Some of my raptor friends' diminished
Numbers also make me wonder,
Whatever happened to the owl
And to the hawk, performers

Of those loud mock battles
In the eucalyptus trees?

Now wispy gray and whitish clouds
Come slowly up across
The blue sky from the south;
Some tower up, as if
To signal thunderstorms.
And now also a modest wind springs up.

Somewhere on earth, perhaps
Life with its rhythms is disturbed,
While heat increases providential warnings here.

Four rosebuds opened on the lawn.
The topmost favors red.
The outermost displays
Her golden innermost content.
The other two blend in.
But each of them claims
And protects the stalk
That holds their beauty
Up to light and wind.
They dance, joined by the swaying
Green leaves on the neighbors' trees,
And by quick ambling wedding flights
Of our black-white butterflies
Around the rose-born tree.

Four roses in the garden gently sway
In rhythmic waves of heat
And wind, gently touching all.
And like the ocean swells to touch the earth,
The four directions touch the universe,

The very dance uniting in the stem
And in the water-bearing root
Of our roses.

The crystal spring of living water
The angel showed to Hagar through her tears,
The living water Ishmael's people
Drink this very day and live.

That living water from the spring
Jesus would offer to his soul friend
Who receives his Spirit and believes in him.
Cool is, and clear, the living water that unites
Four of my garden roses into one.
To life!

Thanks be to God,
Who gives us this clear water.

July 17, 2017

Dear friends far and near: Day by summer day, while the great river valleys bake in the summer's heat, the coastland is blessed with fog, the gift of the ocean. Mindful of you, my friends, who endure the forests aflame, the heat of the sun, enormous squalls of rain, and flash floods, I still want to share with you the blessings of the coastland's morning fog and the dance of the wind in the afternoon. May sanity and peace return to our thoughts and communications. May peaceful thoughts and mutual respect govern the conduct of humanity on earth. That is my prayer. God bless you all.

California Fog

Cool California fog,
like silver summer gauze over
wind, stilled for the moist,
hesitant rising of morning light.

Day by diminishing day,
expecting the sun to rise ever later
as summer drifts toward fall
and day toward night.

But from noon until onset of eve
the fog lifts clear of the land.
Then gently the wind moves
the undulant boughs and
the blue-blossomed bushes
in harmony's height of
the tall eucalyptus branches
that, swaying clear of the fog,
bend and sing with the wind.

From out of their midst
the voice of a mourning dove
sounds, singing a solo lament:
*Where are you, love of my soul. Oh,
oh, where are you hiding, my love?*

So beautiful in the communion of
honey-filled purple-clad flowers,

beautiful rose, red–golden blossom,
you sing in the language of summer
your rhyme for the wind–rushing dance.

Here in the garden I wait
for the uplifting beat of your wings,
their whistling cadences, jubilant
wingbeats, filled with the praises of God!
Ere the sea and the land
at day's end tuck us in
with Mother Earth's soft, loving hand
and with blessings of peace,
fog from the ocean returning
spreads blessings all over the land.

Welcome to the World, Child: Praise

Send praise to springs
from where waters flow,
deep as the soul of life
under eternity's sky, and show
where the temple is furnished
with food made to grow
on this well-watered ground
to the joy of the manifold sounds
of creation.

Give thanks to the One
whom you praise with your song
of ongoing life and love
gifted to carry the human form,
your child,
into the ocean waters of love,
to live your life with us all
not without struggle,
this perilous birth
unto earth.
But welcome, singer of praise.
Be who you are.

Dear friends far and near: While my brain lets go of the troubling freight of rationalized thoughts, the still small voice whispers love and sends that gift by the beak of a little songbird in the morning. I heard it, and so I send it on to all of you: love, the holy gift of life!

Whisper

"Awake?"
the morning whispered.
Bowstring vibrant sound
precedes the first spark
of the light alive above
the westward-sloping Oakland hills.

On Alameda's shores
the whisper and the spark
caught in the eye and ear
of the Holy Spirit,
moving the waves of mighty waters

sent over troubled seas
and deserts filled with fears,
to speak with a commanding
voice of stern authority:
"Cease warfare!"

Learn the morning's whispered song,
which I entrusted
to the little waking voice
of earth creation:
love.
Eternal echo in the human heart.
Learn it and live.

Dear friends far and near: May health and healing be yours, and may you have quiet confidence in the love and care beyond our knowing.

Silence in the Storm

Soft the wind,
still the slowly swaying,
the quiet blossom
congregations on the stalks
of fragrant flowers
in the garden, waiting
for the daylight
slowly filtering through the morning fog.

These all are messengers,
survivors of fierce storms,
of overwhelming floods
delivering news
of waters through
the open sluices of the sky,
and floods of mindless words
bursting through open cracks
of ignorant malevolence,
all of them racing, frightening
human souls that plead for peace.

There enters, adorned
with the light of eternal day,
the Word,
majestic authority,
the word that Noah hears in the storm-tossed ark
and that he obeys as he opens
the door of his soul
for the peace-pleading dove.

With her descends the message from on high:
Proud ignorance,
cease your warfare.
Learn to follow in the path
through cross and death
up to the everlasting light,
your spirit home of fragrant
silent love.
I AM.

Dear friends far and near: Nature, the assemblage of life in whose midst I also live—that is my touchstone. And I enjoy sharing my impressions with you. In the morning, which the earthlight borrows from the Eternal Light, I humbly pray that in its glow we all shall have life and be blessed.

Day Rise

Souls in the morning
working on, waiting for,
their assignment's fulfillment
are actors invited to my stage,
the porch: I greet you one and all.

Mr. and Mrs. Robin Bird
doing their kangaroo hop
over the sidewalk, the garden,
and the neighborhood street.

Titmice, their lively assembly
winging and singing,
done with the squeaks and the chants
of their morning prayers,
now descend on the flowers,
the bushes, the branches,
and the railings and leaves on the porch
to feed on the bugs on the leaves.
The spiders and the mosquitoes they eat.
Life's ample nourishment—
O what a feast!

I breathe in the oxygen, gift
of the conifer bush by the stairs.
He breathes it directly to me.
I breathe out the carbon dioxide
I have been given for him.

Even exchange, mutual soul food,
sustaining our mutual lives
in the rhythm of thanks.

The sun is risen. The promise:
another hot day. The creatures,
leaving the stage, seek out
the merciful shade, as others
are fleeing the deluge of Noah
in search of a little dry place.

These are the ins and
the outs we are given
to work with, rejoicing
and praying to God
for salvation and life
on our planet, the earth.

The Spirit who knows and
sees us all, his creation,
feeds all of us
who give thanks.

Stoop the Stage

How I savor silence,
so evocative of meaning.
I have joined my fellow actors
on the stoop—the stage,
the entrance of my home—
and am here now, inviting all of you
who pass or stay awhile
with me to share your story.

You who exchange the air with me
and you who, rooted in the ground,
display the beauty of creation
topped with the full creation sound
of dancing roses
swaying in the lively wind.

Wind that delivers joy
and sadness to our stage:
the news of frightful storms,
deluges washing out the ground,
washing the shaken human habitation
out into raging, broken land.

But even horror finds its end.
Fear beats retreat. The howling
simmers down and fades
into dark nightmare caves
whence it had come.

Now eastward with the rising sun,
I see the wings of raptors cycling
so steady 'round the groves of gum
in ever strengthening waves of wind.
Above the golfing meadows swung,
so full of elegance and pinion strength,
the busy condors are cleaning up the land.

In flies a squadron of the singing geese
from the lagoon, where they,
in darkness hidden, spent the night.
Their song stays in the air
where they were flying
to settle in the meadows' lushness,
the equals of the little songs and tweets
from garden shrubs and sweets of flowers
where all my feather-winged neighbors
love, nest, and spend their living hours.

From garden grass up to the flowers
fly mini monarch butterflies,
always in pairs, sharing the fragrance
and all the wind-stirred living air,
inviting other newly wing'd arrivals
like the cabbage white in its solo flight.

And—would you know—
I saw aright the rust-red wings
of the monarch butterfly, here
in the sun spot on the lawn close by.
How did they ever cross the wall?
From Mexico they came to bless us all!

My raven neighbors caw alarm.
Just flying in, they heard what I have heard:
the screaming song of a
red-tailed hawk in flight
that promises what they have missed so long—
a playful fight-or-flight dance and raptor's song.

That turns the crows' alarm to mirth,
sounding like little dogs, not birds.
Their cawing sounds like laughing tweets,
like freedom of expression, off the leash
all up and down the neighborhood
and garden paths secure with peace.
Good morning!

Dear friends far and near: You might wonder how in our present stress-laden time a butterfly excites my heart and mind. But here is why: All spring and summer long I missed the sight of the rust-red winged monarch butterfly. The Mexican eucalyptus groves where it winters are rumored to have suffered destruction. Meanwhile a community of black-rimmed white-winged butterflies has filled the monarch's niche in our Alameda neighborhood. I bid them welcome, but I miss the monarchs, California's beautiful rust-red flyers.

Imagine my joy when this morning the monarch came to visit me, as if to tell me to have faith. Life has more ways than one to reassert itself. That is the good news I want to share with you my friends.

Rust-Red Flyer

The sun has come
to bring us light
and promised warmth.
The radio, with its news
of dire dangers,
is turned off.

My stoop stage's
plants and flowers
bend their petals to the sun
and, holding still,
enjoy the quiet morning.

A movement of—yes—
rust-red wings in flight
across the stage
delivers blessings from
the longed-for home:
hope for the day
and faith to trust
the Holy One
who guides the wingbeats
of resilient life.

The monarch crosses now the stage.
He's taking note of the surprising
Christmas flowers, early to appear
as bloodred blossoms, early in the year,

drawing his rapt attention.
But after the inspecting flight is done,
the monarch flies around the corner and is gone.

Now hummingbird,
descending from the tall trees'
shelter down to the stage light
of the sun path monarch left,
tracing its flight, finds
sweet nectar in these early flowers,
the free bestowal of creative might.
Drinks now from that communion drink
and fills its crop with it
to benefit its nestling young
before it reascends onto its home
from where all blessings come.
Thanks be to God.

Dear friends far and near: Even unseen, the monarch butterfly I missed is very real. And so is every unseen soul eternally created changed and blessed, with new tasks sent forth. That faith helps me overcome sad and painful times and helps me to rejoice in the strength of *life* eternally descending from above the mountains the psalmist praises in Psalm 121. Even on the cross that help is here. *Deo gracias.*

Lift Your Eyes

Lift your eyes, O lift your eyes
beyond the mountains of the light,
and sink your heart and soul
into the depth to search the height
and depth for answers to your sighs.

What do you teach us, Lord?
Is every thunder anger?
Is our human comprehension
the measure of all truth?
Is not the word of love
the truth that guides the searching soul?

Do not despair with sadness, O my soul,
but rather look and, listening, learn
from rooted roses, winged birds,
leaves letting go of branches
so that the tree of life can grow
where softly falling leaves now rain
from the shelter tree so quietly
onto the ground above the roots
that once propelled them up so joyously.

From the heights, the mountains of light
are handing the Word to my soul:
Every dew-freshened morning now
floats the Word down in the guise
of a singular butterfly, once

from our neighborhood gone.
But it is he, the beautiful monarch.
He enters and exits the stage of this home,
then briefly floats over the flowers,
kisses the rose in the midst of the lawn,
leaving for all of us blessings of life
as he flies into heights
of eternity.
Thanks be to God.

Dear friends far and near: Inspired by Paul's letter to the Philippians (ch. 3), I opened my mind to thoughts about the law and its manifestations. The contemplation led me to the law chiseled and established in the rock on the sacred mountain, then to the law as written on the sacred scroll to travel with the people wherever they settled on earth. Most amazing is Christ, the law fulfilled in human vesture.

May his blessings guide our every step through life. To you who are suffering the fire's fury, I offer my prayers amid the flood of your tears.

Law, the Guide

Chiseled in Rock,
wisdom the temple,
grounded forever secure.
Guide for the pilgrim's path,
stored on the mountaintop,
light human knowledge can't grasp.

But with prayers ascending
there bursts from the rock sacred water,
slaking the people's thirst
and their hunger for righteousness.

Water and law, gifts from on high
for the soul on the peacemaker's path,
gifts for all thankful creation,
touchstones, the truth of our life.

Lone creatures, ambling butterflies
come to the stage greeting me.
So do the hummingbirds'
green-glistening jewel wings
bring to the morning their greetings
of flowers for Martha at work
and for Mary, the silent beloved.

But woe to the deafening noise
of the warrior jets overhead,
storm-driven fires roaring their threats

of impending disasters,
lawlessly heedless as death.

By all of those threats unperturbed,
our garden frog, newly returned, aims to stay
in our flourishing garden greens,
correcting the compass
and teaching us pilgrims the way:

First of all, find where to anchor your faith.
Next learn what I hear, and then say:
Law is adjusting to all that you need,
expressed in the people's prayer.

The answer to come over deserts and sea,
from heavenly places sent,
arrives among us assuredly.

The ultimate law,
compassion and peace,
redemption and love, is
the Word.

Dear friends far and near: Between Halloween and All Hallows' Eve morning, the unquenchable light of life welcomes each of us to live life mindfully. The costume we wear in the darkening evening, and the one we wash and then wear in the daylight, are both ours. I wear my old man's costume. From where I am assigned to live my life, I think of you with best of thoughts and blessings.

Plea

A cooler wind now
sways the branches.
The leaves, however,
still cling to their trees
like measured thoughts,
using eyes and mind
and time to take
the temperature of our life
on earth.

But human brains,
placed by some chance
into high places,
dig in obscure
heated puddles of
malignant feelings.
Then throw mud by the handful
wildly in the round,
until they have
the war they want to use
for aimless, thoughtless
life destruction.

Have mercy, Lord,
we pray.
Thank you for angel–teachers
coming to our aid,

and at your bidding
blessing us.
Amen.
Amen.

Veronica Love

You, offspring of the Inca ancestors,
Messiah-love of God
from the beginning,
arisen from dark mountain canyons
on condor wings of love
onto the Pampas and the ocean waves.

I love you—love your smile
that spreads the peace of God
all over this fair coastland
where our eyes first met. And I've
remembered ever since the time
when our souls met
and our love assumed a different form.

Your name, however,
was already in my heart,
as mild as Sunday-evening sunshine,
strong as the blessings of
Lord Christ,
who loves you
and graciously chose me to be the man
to say,
"Veronica, I love you from my heart."
God bless your life.

Dear friends: All gifts come from the Spirit. The most beautiful of all these gifts is love. May it bless us all and grant us peace.

Tears to Learn By

The season of cool nights
still gives the light,
from sunup to the peace
of farewell rituals,
their tearful orderly content.

The twilight holds all creatures
of the neighborhood, gently embraced,
gently unclasping hands
from hands and feet from feet
with tender care—
my heart from yours,
your soul from mine.

With time and distance overcome,
we open our eyes
and see eternal love
walk into night with us.

To be reborn with resurrected light:
the farewell with the tears that Peter cried.
The morning reveille with tears of grace
that baptized Mary Magdalene
with love
beyond the grave.

Dear friends far and near: I recently received a friendly admonition I'd first received years ago from Hella Jaensch, my mother. I think it is worth sharing with you all here: "Take care," she said. "Sacred references can get overused." I do remember. The quiet moment is the Presence.

Cross in the Clouds

A horizontal cross:
It plies the waves of air.
No sail is bulging in the wind
above this friendly neighborhood.
Wings of aluminum
pressed forth with motor noise
lift up a pilot and
a student with him in the plane
atop a wall of air
measured with instruments,
and onto waves
of sun-filled clarity.

A pair of human eyes
has noticed how the eagle flies.
They now can also fly,
but fill the air with noise.

Hawk with his wings spread wide
approaches low tall trees
above the golfing greens,
Australian natives blossoming
profusely with the memory
of outback spring at home.

Sweeps up, takes hold
of swaying bows high up.
Among the blossoms now

he's resting quietly,
and with unfailing sight
he looks on the earth
with love.

My dear friends far and near: Wars and rumors of war can be witnessed with a click of the radio dial. I am not in denial. The tide of pain and tears grows day by day.

But I was given a reassuring vision of safety and peace last night at our little Crab Cove here in Alameda, California. I want to share that with you and send it to you with blessings.

Crab Cove Compline

Mirror-smooth,
so clear far out to sea,
down to the pebbled ground
the water mirrors gray
the barely moving evening clouds.

This cove seldom appears
so clean and clear
to all the water creatures far and near,
or to the crows that venture
out to rows of rocks.
And there they stay awhile
out in the quiet eventide,
enjoying the hospitality
of the peaceful air below,
the darkling westward drifting light.

Immense the distance
open to the eye, and
to the ear the symphony
of sounds from clouds
of shorebirds swiftly
flying by and landing
on the bay shore's other side.

A pelican flies low
above the surface of the bay,
unhurried wingbeat but

surprising swift its forward flow.
Now on the rocks below
a nervous bird has landed.
Now he takes off again,
lands on another rock,
to rise once more and
land on yet another rock
on shore.

A smaller bird, of sparrow's size,
now taking off from shore
above a water whirlpool, flies
round and round and round once more.
And yet once more around she flies
until the water—cleared—
allows a single rock to rise,
just like the dove of Noah flew and found
the rock, the landing, the dry ground.

Now she stays here.
The coots swim over, slow,
to check the rock,
checking the black and silver bird on top,
then take a beak of seaweed
and swim on.

All eyes wait for the Lord
to lower evening light and tide,
until it's time to feed
all creatures with the best
that Mother Earth provides
for their well-being.

Blest be the land, the sea,
the setting light of day.
Thanks be to God
for life.
Amen.
Thanks for a peaceful day.

Anna in the Temple

The morning light arises.
From the east it visits us
And fills our coastland
With the eager expectation
Of our longing hearts,
With glorious holiness seen
By Ezekiel, the prophet,
Which filled the temple then.

This morning it filled Anna's heart,
Although so many years had passed.
Time counts for little in the presence
of the Holy One.
Each day Messiah rises from the east
To visit ready hearts, like Anna's.
With knowledge: He is here!
She hastens to the temple,
Greeting with each stride
Of every step the child
Who, in the arms of Simeon,
Receives the human welcome
To the temple, and the blessing
Earth received from God
In the beginning.

This Christmas morning
My heart is just as ready
As was Anna's then,

Looking upon this neighborhood
Where all creation now is,
Sleeping or awake, alive,
As Anna's was the morning
When the Lord arrived
A child to fill the temple
With creation's light.

Christmas 2017

News from Earth

The steam from the neighbor's roof,
Translucent wisp of gray,
Ascending to the morning height,
While birds, although equipped for flight,
Collect their breakfast from the ground,

Examining each blade of grass in search
Of food, to follow what it learned in school.
It finds where food is found.

I also search for the food I need to live
Where morning light arises and resides,
Where the ascending spirit guides,
Until I, face-to-face, have found
The unassailable abode of life
I hunger for:
The love of Christ.

December 1, 2017

Green Christmas Light

Is this the morning light
Observed the way young Andersen
Observed the mermaid
And how she, so filled with longing,
Experienced Christmas in the
Wintry frost of Denmark's sea?

Green branches at my bright
Pacific home remind me
Of that early vision, of
The Baltic Sea with sacrifices filled:

Green-leafed camellias,
Rhododendron in the light,
Abode of joy-filled blossoms,
Bliss of love, a nesting place
For sparrow and for dove
And for the brindled bird.
She saw them in the sunlight
Up above on this fair
Christmas Day's arrival
Of Jesus, child of Mary,
Son of God.
And sacrificed it all for love.

The mermaid, looking longingly
From Copenhagen's harbor bay,
With love the content of her heart,

Bade welcome to the child's descent
To a shepherd's field in Bethlehem—
This sacrifice of holy love
All for the sake of darkened minds—
Then made her own descent
Into the swaying green. Like
Magdalen she sacrificed
The love she has for Christ
For you and me.

The Hoot

The longest night
Already came and passed along
The stony path and fruitful ground
Where sheep and goats find grazing.
The lion also finds his food source, watched
By shepherds, who make sure
All of creation takes and eats enough.

To live with reverence to
The One,
The grand mysterious sound.
Sovereign of ending and beginning,
The sound the mighty oceans heard
And stopped, advancing on good Mother Earth.

Also in flyways of the earth
The sound was heard by all the winged ones:
The birds, the butterflies, and all the angels
Sent to accompany the One
To whom all hearts are open
And all secrets are known.

Unseen by night-light at his grand descent
Down to the tallest trees of our neighborhood,
He landed and announced,
"I bless you all.
I give that hoot

For all I do create
And call it good from the beginning.
The call fills earth with my compassion."
Unseen but heard:
The music of the spheres,
The song of love.

"This is for me and you,"
Said monarch butterfly,
And brindled sparrow, too.

Amazing Valentine

The flautist section seated,
Rehearsed, and tuned, now
Sings in harmony the true
Song of the red-winged blackbird.

Welcome back to our neighborhood!
From where you hid, survived
The ravens' grand invasion
And muting of your song.

Paper in hand, I straighten up,
Survey the branches of your tree:
In this fair morning light,
I count only one, two, three ...

Six of you musicians making melody
As soft, as strong, as your community
Were singing when the as yet
Prespringtime leafless swaying tree

Was filled with jubilant
Harmonious praise to our Creator,
One grand impressive
Solid faith crescendo,
The model of success for all ...

God listened to the ravens, too,
The sparrows and the garden frogs,

The little singers singing
With mighty voices their praise,
Enveloping the sight of rose
Called love,
Beloved of Creator's heart.

February 1, 2018

Dear friends far and near: Each morning I notice with joy the return to my neighborhood of fellow creatures I'd thought lost and gone: the monarch butterfly, the red-winged blackbird ... They have returned, albeit in numbers much reduced. There is a lesson here we humans ought to learn and keep in mind: We Californians face another year of drought. We humans tell each other not to worry, saying the reservoirs still overflow with water.

Our fellow creatures also felt the warning we'd received. Reduced in numbers, they sing songs of returning, carrying their sheaves of adequate harvests that will bless us all. Thanks be to God.

A Special Highway

Ere yet the sun brightened the morning sky.
Familiar motor sounds of different decibels,
along with squeaks and wake-up sounds,
were issuing from lawns and shrubs and trees.

One voice stood out: The red-tailed hawk
announced his presence with his cleats
before he left the grove of shelter trees.
Crows left him to his flight. They knew
he would be back for his accustomed fight.

The small musicians paid attention
but, knowing that he'd flown away,
commenced their praises to the light of day.
High up where eucalyptus branches,
their leaves and blossoms, sway
is a portrait of a thankful prayer
for birthing this new day.

High up the raptor flies,
in view of all the universe.
His wings cut spirals through
untroubled blue folds of the sky.
Above where eucalyptus branches,
leaves, blossoms, lawns, and roses
frame my eyes' and ears' reality,
once more I see him fly his circle.
Then he disappears, but only
from the limit of my sight.

High in the noontime,
pinions stretched, you fly,
proving the air you cycle,
the air that all of us creatures breathe,
is reliable and worthy of our trust.

Your flight sends signals from above
to us who follow after.
We creatures try to hear past noise
of cars and planes your will expressed.

Four crows appear and, cawing,
rise with ambling wingbeats,
landing on the tops of wires,
when our garden frog
awakes and loudly sings
some stanzas of his song.

The hawk's majestic flight, inaudible,
invisible to us, continues on.
A signal to us actors on this stage
is heard and understood ...

The bidding prayer done,
my neighbors quit their song.
I return to listening now
to silence.

The Rose and the Frog

The rose,
The only one to open red,
Her petals to the rising sun.
All other branches carry leaves
Alone with slow advance
Into the cool bright morning.

The queen of roses dances
To songs of a garden frog
Who seeks the favor of his mate,
But rose accepts the song
As equally unique.

Neither the solo frog
Nor she has heard
The choral symphony
Of those still underground,
Until the grand rain
Frees their joyful jubilation.

February 10, 2018

Dear friends far and near: I am profoundly thankful that I am still judged worthy and useful as an instrument to sing praises to God. I like to share these praises with you in gratitude for your friendship and affection.

Endurance

Let down the blinds, entrust
Prakrit-nature to the all-
creating One in whom
you rest your faith, my soul.

The One Almighty, silent One,
who overrules persistent whisperings,
disturbing dreams, faint fears—
scrapes of camellia's leaf and branch
whipping against the window and the wall
with strong, cold wind, dry rays
of westward-moving sun.

I wonder where the little occupants
of wind-whipped branches spend this night
and how the rose, the singular assurance
of the life, now turned from red
to beige, to old from young,
in this storm wind is hanging on
with strength-of-faith resilience.

Will she still be alive when morning dawns?

The morning light subdued the storm.
The little neighbors, sparrows, finches,
had breakfast on the dew-fresh lawn.
The cleats of hawk, the caws of crows,
sent greetings from the tall trees'

swaying crowns down to my garden stage,
where rose, the much beloved,
dances gratitude for strength of faith
that held on to the vine all night
and is alive today.

The Cat

Beautiful cat.
Her smooth fur shines
when her paws walk
to carry her up
the sun-lighted driveway, alert!

Now the cat lifts her face
up to where the bird just intoned
her melodious warning.
Cat knows I sit here and watch,
but her eyes stab and embrace
the bird's song alone.
Nothing else
is.

She wants to see movement
enticing her, ready to jump.
All sound is dismissed.
Silence alone sways softly
the rose in the garden.

Printed in the United States
By Bookmasters